THAT LITTLE GAME

Bert Link

THAT LITTLE GAME

Bert Link

Bert Link

Editor: Chad Arment

Coachwhip Publications
Landisville, Pennsylvania

Copyright © 2004. All rights reserved.

Published by Coachwhip Publications.

                        Publisher's Cataloging-in-Publication Data

Link, Bert.

    That little game / Bert Link. — 1st ed. — Landisville, Pa. : Coachwhip Publications, 2004.

    p. ; cm.

    Summary: A collection of 1920s newspaper comic panels focused on poker and similar card games.
    ISBN: 1-930585-17-9

    1. Poker—Comic books, strips, etc. 2. Poker—Humor. 3. Card games—Comic books, strips, etc. 4. Card games—Humor. 5. Comic books, strips, etc. I. Title.

PN6728.T438 L56 2004
741.5/973—dc22   CIP

The year is 1920 ...

Prohibition becomes law ...

Women win the right to vote ...

And the entertainment of choice is ...

That Little Game

"THAT LITTLE GAME" === === When A Bluff Went Across

"THAT LITTLE GAME" === === Gummed Up By An Outsider

"THAT LITTLE GAME" === === Etiquette Cuts No Ice

"THAT LITTLE GAME" === === The Apron String Still Holds

77

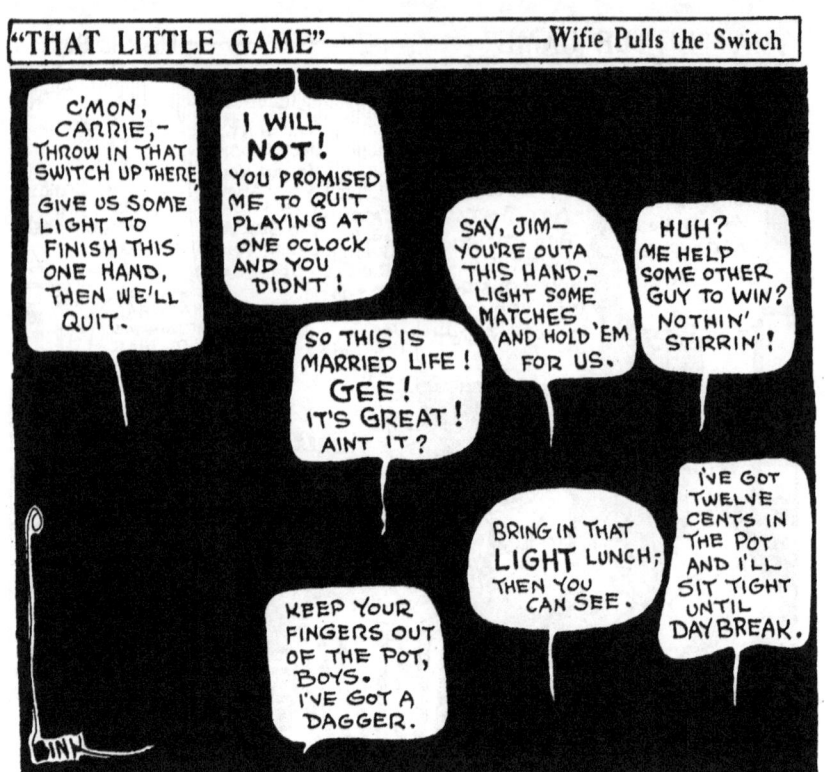

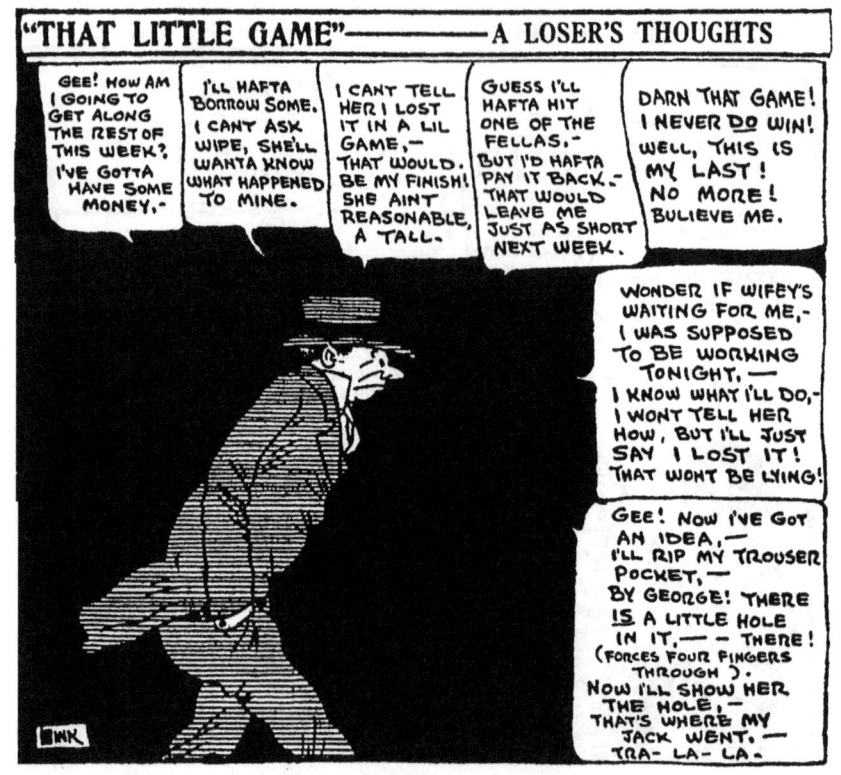

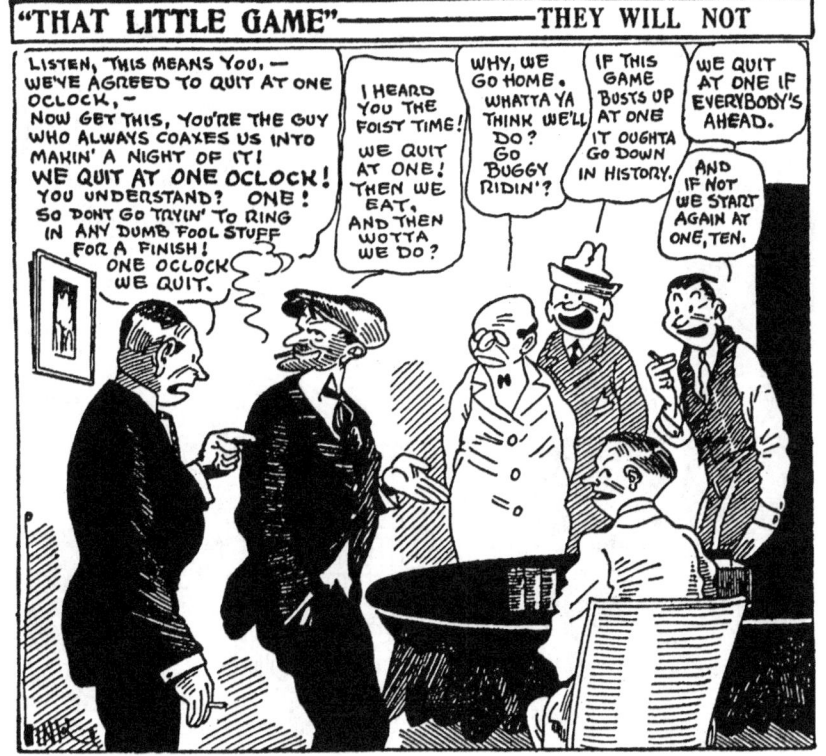

About This Book

"That Little Game" ran from approximately 1917 to 1927. This collection includes comic panels which ran in *The Lancaster Daily Intelligencer* (PA) in 1920.

Bert Link's other published comics included "One Reel" and "Movie Strips."

The current editor's intent was to present these panels in a clean legible format while accurately depicting the original detailed artwork. In some cases, poor preservation did not allow for completeness.

Thanks to Leonardo De Sa for information on the publication dates.

www.ingramcontent.com/pod-product-compliance
Lightning Source LLC
LaVergne TN
LVHW061345060426
835512LV00012B/2572